MW01527810

RV Log Book

©2015 by Wandering Walks of Wonder Publishing

Printed in the United States of America

All rights reserved. No part of this work covered by the copyrights hereon may be reproduced or used in any form or by any means – graphic, electronic or mechanical – without the prior written permission of the publishers, except for reviewers who may quote brief passages. Any request for photocopying, recording, taping or storage on information retrieval systems of any part of this work shall be directed in writing to the publisher.

The Publisher: Wandering Walks of Wonder Publishing

Kansas City, MO 64118

USA

Website: www.wanderingwalksofwonder.com

ISBN-13: 978-1514874929

ISBN-10: 151487492X

This Journal

Belongs to:

_____

_____

Keeping a journal to chronicle events has declined over time. Years ago, journals were common place. Many famous events were written down. Like Anne Frank and her diary. She kept up with what was going on with her family during two years of hiding. What about Lewis and Clark and their expedition? Yes, there is great detail in their adventure. They made over 140 maps and documents local plant and animal species.

Okay, so you don't want to write about that much detail in your journal. But, it might be nice to be able to look back on some of the RV Camping trips that you have been on in the past.

This journal provides plenty of space to write your thoughts about each camp site and camp location you take.

One final thought is that you should write in your journal while you are on the road. Don't leave it up to, "I will remember that when I get home." Chances are you won't remember.

Camping is a great way to get back in touch with a slower pace of life. The experiences while performing these activities are endless. Writing in a journal makes them timeless.

Date of Trip:	Location of Campsite:
	Park Name_____
	Campground Name_____
	Campsite Number_____
	City/State_____

Weather:	Mileage:	Expenses:
☀ ⛅ 🌧 🌨	Today's Beginning Mileage_____ Today's Ending Mileage_____ Total Miles Driven_____	Gas $_____ Food $_____ Supplies $_____ Other $_____

Campground Details:

_____

_____

_____

_____

_____

Campsite Details:

_____

_____

_____

_____

_____

_____

_____

Activities Offered:

_____

_____

_____

_____

_____

Things I did:

_____

_____

_____

_____

_____

Flora and Fauna I saw:

_____

_____

_____

_____

_____

What I liked most about this Trip:

_____

_____

_____

_____

_____

Date of Trip:	Location of Campsite:	
	Park Name_____	
	Campground Name_____	
	Campsite Number_____	
	City/State_____	

Weather:	Mileage:	Expenses:
☼ ⛅ ☁ ☃	Today's Beginning Mileage_____ Today's Ending Mileage_____ Total Miles Driven_____	Gas $_____ Food $_____ Supplies $_____ Other $_____

Campground Details:

_____

_____

_____

_____

_____

Campsite Details:

_____

_____

_____

_____

_____

_____

_____

Activities Offered:

_____

_____

_____

_____

Things I did:

_____

_____

_____

_____

Flora and Fauna I saw:

_____

_____

_____

_____

What I liked most about this Trip:

_____

_____

_____

_____

Date of Trip:	Location of Campsite:	
	Park Name_____	
	Campground Name_____	
	Campsite Number_____	
	City/State_____	

Weather:	Mileage:	Expenses:
☀ ⛅ 🌧 🌨	Today's Beginning Mileage_____ Today's Ending Mileage_____ Total Miles Driven_____	Gas $_____ Food $_____ Supplies $_____ Other $_____

Campground Details:

_____
_____
_____
_____
_____

Campsite Details:

_____
_____
_____
_____
_____
_____
_____

Activities Offered:

_____

_____

_____

_____

Things I did:

_____

_____

_____

_____

Flora and Fauna I saw:

_____

_____

_____

_____

What I liked most about this Trip:

_____

_____

_____

_____

_____

Date of Trip:	Location of Campsite: Park Name_____ Campground Name_____ Campsite Number_____ City/State_____	
Weather: ☀ ⛅ 🌧 🌨	Mileage: Today's Beginning Mileage_____ Today's Ending Mileage_____ Total Miles Driven_____	Expenses: Gas $_____ Food $_____ Supplies $_____ Other $_____

Campground Details:

_____

_____

_____

_____

_____

Campsite Details:

_____

_____

_____

_____

_____

_____

_____

Activities Offered:

_____

_____

_____

_____

_____

Things I did:

_____

_____

_____

_____

_____

Flora and Fauna I saw:

_____

_____

_____

_____

_____

What I liked most about this Trip:

_____

_____

_____

_____

_____

Date of Trip:	Location of Campsite:	
	Park Name_____	
	Campground Name_____	
	Campsite Number_____	
	City/State_____	

Weather:	Mileage:	Expenses:
☀ ⛅ ☁ 🌧	Today's Beginning Mileage_____ Today's Ending Mileage_____ Total Miles Driven_____	Gas $_____ Food $_____ Supplies $_____ Other $_____

Campground Details:

_____

_____

_____

_____

_____

Campsite Details:

_____

_____

_____

_____

_____

_____

_____

Activities Offered:

_____

_____

_____

_____

Things I did:

_____

_____

_____

_____

Flora and Fauna I saw:

_____

_____

_____

_____

What I liked most about this Trip:

_____

_____

_____

_____

Date of Trip:	Location of Campsite:
	Park Name_____
	Campground Name_____
	Campsite Number_____
	City/State_____

Weather:	Mileage:	Expenses:
☀ ⛅ ☁ 🌧	Today's Beginning Mileage_____ Today's Ending Mileage_____ Total Miles Driven_____	Gas $_____ Food $_____ Supplies $_____ Other $_____

Campground Details:

_____

_____

_____

_____

_____

Campsite Details:

_____

_____

_____

_____

_____

_____

Activities Offered:

_____

_____

_____

_____

Things I did:

_____

_____

_____

_____

Flora and Fauna I saw:

_____

_____

_____

_____

What I liked most about this Trip:

_____

_____

_____

_____

Date of Trip:	Location of Campsite:
	Park Name_____
	Campground Name_____
	Campsite Number_____
	City/State_____

Weather:	Mileage:	Expenses:
☀ ⛅ ☁ 🌧 🌨	Today's Beginning Mileage_____ Today's Ending Mileage_____ Total Miles Driven_____	Gas $_____ Food $_____ Supplies $_____ Other $_____

Campground Details:

_____
_____
_____
_____
_____

Campsite Details:

_____
_____
_____
_____
_____
_____
_____

Activities Offered:

_____

_____

_____

_____

_____

Things I did:

_____

_____

_____

_____

_____

Flora and Fauna I saw:

_____

_____

_____

_____

_____

What I liked most about this Trip:

_____

_____

_____

_____

_____

Date of Trip:	Location of Campsite:	
	Park Name_____	
	Campground Name_____	
	Campsite Number_____	
	City/State_____	

Weather:	Mileage:	Expenses:
☀ ⛅	Today's Beginning Mileage_____	Gas $_____
☁ 🌨	Today's Ending Mileage_____	Food $_____
	Total Miles Driven_____	Supplies $_____
		Other $_____

Campground Details:

_____

_____

_____

_____

_____

Campsite Details:

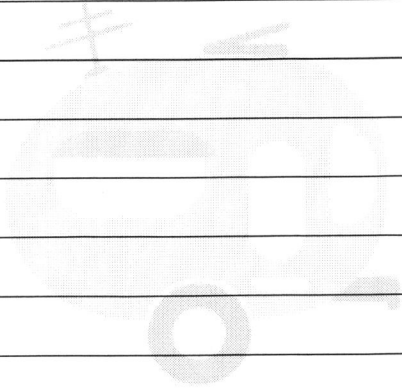

_____

_____

_____

_____

_____

_____

_____

Activities Offered:

_____

_____

_____

_____

Things I did:

_____

_____

_____

_____

Flora and Fauna I saw:

_____

_____

_____

_____

What I liked most about this Trip:

_____

_____

_____

_____

Date of Trip:	Location of Campsite: Park Name_____ Campground Name_____ Campsite Number_____ City/State_____	
Weather: ☀ ⛅ 🌧 🌨	Mileage: Today's Beginning Mileage_____ Today's Ending Mileage_____ Total Miles Driven_____	Expenses: Gas $_____ Food $_____ Supplies $_____ Other $_____

Campground Details:

_____

_____

_____

_____

_____

Campsite Details:

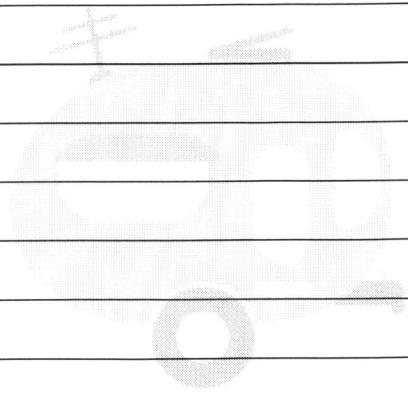

_____

_____

_____

_____

_____

_____

_____

Activities Offered:

_____

_____

_____

_____

Things I did:

_____

_____

_____

_____

Flora and Fauna I saw:

_____

_____

_____

_____

What I liked most about this Trip:

_____

_____

_____

_____

Date of Trip:	Location of Campsite:
	Park Name_____
	Campground Name_____
	Campsite Number_____
	City/State_____

Weather:	Mileage:	Expenses:
☀ ⛅ ☁ 🌧	Today's Beginning Mileage_____	Gas $_____
	Today's Ending Mileage_____	Food $_____
	Total Miles Driven_____	Supplies $_____
		Other $_____

Campground Details:

_____

_____

_____

_____

_____

Campsite Details:

_____

_____

_____

_____

_____

_____

_____

Activities Offered:

_____

_____

_____

_____

Things I did:

_____

_____

_____

_____

Flora and Fauna I saw:

_____

_____

_____

_____

What I liked most about this Trip:

_____

_____

_____

_____

Date of Trip:	Location of Campsite:	
	Park Name_____	
	Campground Name_____	
	Campsite Number_____	
	City/State_____	

Weather:	Mileage:	Expenses:
☀ ⛅ 🌧 🌨	Today's Beginning Mileage_____ Today's Ending Mileage_____ Total Miles Driven_____	Gas $_____ Food $_____ Supplies $_____ Other $_____

Campground Details:

_____

_____

_____

_____

_____

Campsite Details:

_____

_____

_____

_____

_____

_____

_____

Activities Offered:

_____

_____

_____

_____

_____

Things I did:

_____

_____

_____

_____

_____

Flora and Fauna I saw:

_____

_____

_____

_____

_____

What I liked most about this Trip:

_____

_____

_____

_____

_____

Date of Trip:	Location of Campsite:
	Park Name_____
	Campground Name_____
	Campsite Number_____
	City/State_____

Weather:	Mileage:	Expenses:
☀ ⛅ ☁ 🌧	Today's Beginning Mileage_____ Today's Ending Mileage_____ Total Miles Driven_____	Gas $_____ Food $_____ Supplies $_____ Other $_____

Campground Details:

_____
_____
_____
_____
_____

Campsite Details:

_____
_____
_____
_____
_____
_____
_____

Activities Offered:

_____

_____

_____

_____

Things I did:

_____

_____

_____

_____

Flora and Fauna I saw:

_____

_____

_____

_____

What I liked most about this Trip:

_____

_____

_____

_____

Date of Trip:	Location of Campsite:
	Park Name_____
	Campground Name_____
	Campsite Number_____
	City/State_____

Weather:	Mileage:	Expenses:
☀ ⛅ ☁ 🌧	Today's Beginning Mileage_____ Today's Ending Mileage_____ Total Miles Driven_____	Gas $_____ Food $_____ Supplies $_____ Other $_____

Campground Details:

_____

_____

_____

_____

_____

Campsite Details:

_____

_____

_____

_____

_____

_____

_____

Activities Offered:

_____

_____

_____

_____

_____

Things I did:

_____

_____

_____

_____

_____

Flora and Fauna I saw:

_____

_____

_____

_____

_____

What I liked most about this Trip:

_____

_____

_____

_____

_____

_____

Date of Trip:	Location of Campsite:
	Park Name_____
	Campground Name_____
	Campsite Number_____
	City/State_____

Weather:	Mileage:	Expenses:
☀ ⛅ ☁ 🌧	Today's Beginning Mileage_____	Gas $_____
	Today's Ending Mileage_____	Food $_____
	Total Miles Driven_____	Supplies $_____
		Other $_____

Campground Details:

_____

_____

_____

_____

_____

Campsite Details:

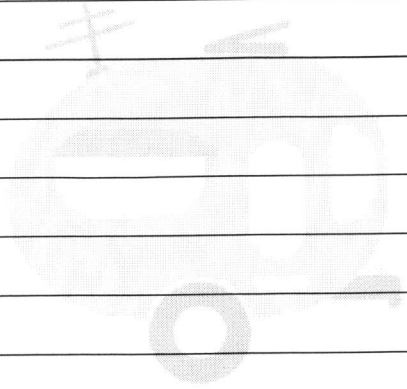

_____

_____

_____

_____

_____

_____

Activities Offered:

_____
_____
_____
_____

Things I did:

_____
_____
_____
_____

Flora and Fauna I saw:

_____
_____
_____
_____

What I liked most about this Trip:

_____
_____
_____
_____

Date of Trip:	Location of Campsite:
	Park Name_____
	Campground Name_____
	Campsite Number_____
	City/State_____

Weather:	Mileage:	Expenses:
☀ ⛅ 🌧 🌨	Today's Beginning Mileage_____ Today's Ending Mileage_____ Total Miles Driven_____	Gas $_____ Food $_____ Supplies $_____ Other $_____

Campground Details:

_____

_____

_____

_____

_____

Campsite Details:

_____

_____

_____

_____

_____

_____

Activities Offered:

_____

_____

_____

_____

Things I did:

_____

_____

_____

_____

Flora and Fauna I saw:

_____

_____

_____

_____

What I liked most about this Trip:

_____

_____

_____

_____

Date of Trip:	Location of Campsite:
	Park Name_____
	Campground Name_____
	Campsite Number_____
	City/State_____

Weather:	Mileage:	Expenses:
☀ ⛅ ☁ 🌧	Today's Beginning Mileage_____ Today's Ending Mileage_____ Total Miles Driven_____	Gas $_____ Food $_____ Supplies $_____ Other $_____

Campground Details:

_____

_____

_____

_____

_____

Campsite Details:

_____

_____

_____

_____

_____

_____

_____

Activities Offered:

_____

_____

_____

_____

Things I did:

_____

_____

_____

_____

Flora and Fauna I saw:

_____

_____

_____

_____

What I liked most about this Trip:

_____

_____

_____

_____

Date of Trip:	Location of Campsite:	
	Park Name_____	
	Campground Name_____	
	Campsite Number_____	
	City/State_____	

Weather:	Mileage:	Expenses:
☀ ⛅ 🌧 🌨	Today's Beginning Mileage_____ Today's Ending Mileage_____ Total Miles Driven_____	Gas $_____ Food $_____ Supplies $_____ Other $_____

Campground Details:

_____

_____

_____

_____

_____

Campsite Details:

_____

_____

_____

_____

_____

_____

_____

Activities Offered:

_____

_____

_____

_____

_____

Things I did:

_____

_____

_____

_____

_____

Flora and Fauna I saw:

_____

_____

_____

_____

_____

What I liked most about this Trip:

_____

_____

_____

_____

_____

Date of Trip:	Location of Campsite:
	Park Name_____
	Campground Name_____
	Campsite Number_____
	City/State_____

Weather:	Mileage:	Expenses:
☀ ⛅ 🌧 🌨	Today's Beginning Mileage_____ Today's Ending Mileage_____ Total Miles Driven_____	Gas $_____ Food $_____ Supplies $_____ Other $_____

Campground Details:

_____

_____

_____

_____

_____

Campsite Details:

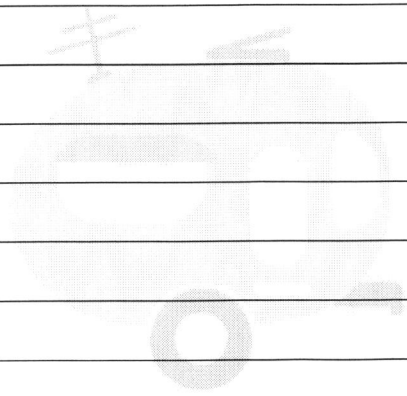

_____

_____

_____

_____

_____

_____

_____

Activities Offered:

_____

_____

_____

_____

Things I did:

_____

_____

_____

_____

Flora and Fauna I saw:

_____

_____

_____

_____

What I liked most about this Trip:

_____

_____

_____

_____

Date of Trip:	Location of Campsite:	
	Park Name_____	
	Campground Name_____	
	Campsite Number_____	
	City/State_____	

Weather:	Mileage:	Expenses:
☀ ⛅ ☁ ☁	Today's Beginning Mileage_____	Gas $_____
	Today's Ending Mileage_____	Food $_____
	Total Miles Driven_____	Supplies $_____
		Other $_____

Campground Details:

_____

_____

_____

_____

_____

Campsite Details:

_____

_____

_____

_____

_____

_____

_____

Activities Offered:

_____

_____

_____

_____

Things I did:

_____

_____

_____

_____

Flora and Fauna I saw:

_____

_____

_____

_____

What I liked most about this Trip:

_____

_____

_____

_____

Date of Trip:	Location of Campsite:	
	Park Name_____	
	Campground Name_____	
	Campsite Number_____	
	City/State_____	

Weather:	Mileage:	Expenses:
☀ ⛅ ☁ 🌧	Today's Beginning Mileage_____	Gas $_____
	Today's Ending Mileage_____	Food $_____
	Total Miles Driven_____	Supplies $_____
		Other $_____

Campground Details:

_____

_____

_____

_____

_____

Campsite Details:

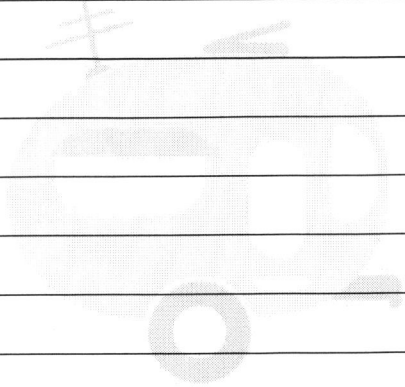

_____

_____

_____

_____

_____

_____

Activities Offered:

_____

_____

_____

_____

Things I did:

_____

_____

_____

_____

Flora and Fauna I saw:

_____

_____

_____

_____

What I liked most about this Trip:

_____

_____

_____

_____

Date of Trip:	Location of Campsite:
	Park Name_____
	Campground Name_____
	Campsite Number_____
	City/State_____

Weather:	Mileage:	Expenses:
☀ ⛅ ☔ ❄	Today's Beginning Mileage_____ Today's Ending Mileage_____ Total Miles Driven_____	Gas $_____ Food $_____ Supplies $_____ Other $_____

Campground Details:

_____
_____
_____
_____
_____
_____

Campsite Details:

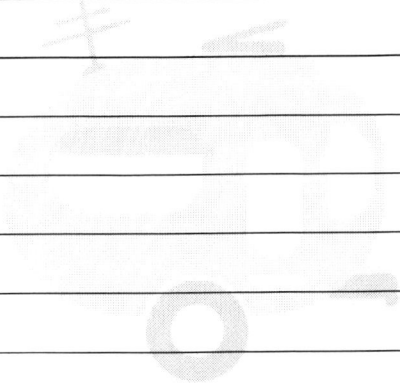

_____
_____
_____
_____
_____
_____
_____
_____

Activities Offered:

_____

_____

_____

_____

_____

Things I did:

_____

_____

_____

_____

_____

Flora and Fauna I saw:

_____

_____

_____

_____

_____

What I liked most about this Trip:

_____

_____

_____

_____

_____

Date of Trip:	Location of Campsite:
	Park Name_____
	Campground Name_____
	Campsite Number_____
	City/State_____

Weather:	Mileage:	Expenses:
☀ ⛅ ☁ ☔	Today's Beginning Mileage_____ Today's Ending Mileage_____ Total Miles Driven_____	Gas $_____ Food $_____ Supplies $_____ Other $_____

Campground Details:

_____

_____

_____

_____

_____

Campsite Details:

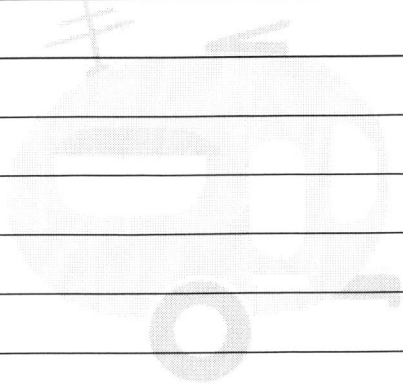

_____

_____

_____

_____

_____

_____

_____

Activities Offered:

_____

_____

_____

_____

Things I did:

_____

_____

_____

_____

Flora and Fauna I saw:

_____

_____

_____

_____

What I liked most about this Trip:

_____

_____

_____

_____

Date of Trip:	Location of Campsite:	
	Park Name_____	
	Campground Name_____	
	Campsite Number_____	
	City/State_____	

Weather:	Mileage:	Expenses:
☀ ⛅ 🌧 🌨	Today's Beginning Mileage_____ Today's Ending Mileage_____ Total Miles Driven_____	Gas $_____ Food $_____ Supplies $_____ Other $_____

Campground Details:

_____

_____

_____

_____

_____

Campsite Details:

_____

_____

_____

_____

_____

_____

_____

Activities Offered:

_____

_____

_____

_____

Things I did:

_____

_____

_____

_____

Flora and Fauna I saw:

_____

_____

_____

_____

What I liked most about this Trip:

_____

_____

_____

_____

Date of Trip:	Location of Campsite:	
	Park Name_____	
	Campground Name_____	
	Campsite Number_____	
	City/State_____	

Weather:	Mileage:	Expenses:
☀ ⛅ ☁ ☃	Today's Beginning Mileage_____ Today's Ending Mileage_____ Total Miles Driven_____	Gas $_____ Food $_____ Supplies $_____ Other $_____

Campground Details:

_____

_____

_____

_____

_____

Campsite Details:

_____

_____

_____

_____

_____

_____

Activities Offered:

_____

_____

_____

_____

Things I did:

_____

_____

_____

_____

Flora and Fauna I saw:

_____

_____

_____

_____

What I liked most about this Trip:

_____

_____

_____

_____

_____

Date of Trip:	Location of Campsite:	
	Park Name_____	
	Campground Name_____	
	Campsite Number_____	
	City/State_____	
Weather:	Mileage:	Expenses:
☀ ⛅ ☁ ☁	Today's Beginning Mileage_____ Today's Ending Mileage_____ Total Miles Driven_____	Gas $_____ Food $_____ Supplies $_____ Other $_____

Campground Details:

_____
_____
_____
_____
_____

Campsite Details:

_____
_____
_____
_____
_____
_____
_____

Activities Offered:

_____

_____

_____

_____

Things I did:

_____

_____

_____

_____

Flora and Fauna I saw:

_____

_____

_____

_____

What I liked most about this Trip:

_____

_____

_____

_____

Date of Trip:	Location of Campsite:
	Park Name_____
	Campground Name_____
	Campsite Number_____
	City/State_____

Weather:	Mileage:	Expenses:
☀ ⛅ ☔ ☁	Today's Beginning Mileage_____ Today's Ending Mileage_____ Total Miles Driven_____	Gas $_____ Food $_____ Supplies $_____ Other $_____

Campground Details:

_____

_____

_____

_____

_____

Campsite Details:

_____

_____

_____

_____

_____

_____

_____

Activities Offered:

_____

_____

_____

_____

Things I did:

_____

_____

_____

_____

Flora and Fauna I saw:

_____

_____

_____

_____

What I liked most about this Trip:

_____

_____

_____

_____

_____

Date of Trip:	Location of Campsite:
	Park Name_____
	Campground Name_____
	Campsite Number_____
	City/State_____

Weather:	Mileage:	Expenses:
☀ ⛅ ☔ ☁	Today's Beginning Mileage_____	Gas $_____
	Today's Ending Mileage_____	Food $_____
	Total Miles Driven_____	Supplies $_____
		Other $_____

Campground Details:

_____

_____

_____

_____

_____

Campsite Details:

_____

_____

_____

_____

_____

_____

_____

Activities Offered:

_____

_____

_____

_____

Things I did:

_____

_____

_____

_____

Flora and Fauna I saw:

_____

_____

_____

_____

What I liked most about this Trip:

_____

_____

_____

_____

_____

Date of Trip:	Location of Campsite:	
	Park Name_____	
	Campground Name_____	
	Campsite Number_____	
	City/State_____	

Weather:	Mileage:	Expenses:
☀ ⛅	Today's Beginning Mileage_____	Gas $_____
	Today's Ending Mileage_____	Food $_____
🌧 🌨	Total Miles Driven_____	Supplies $_____
		Other $_____

Campground Details:

_____
_____
_____
_____
_____

Campsite Details:

_____
_____
_____
_____
_____
_____
_____

Activities Offered:

_____

_____

_____

_____

Things I did:

_____

_____

_____

_____

Flora and Fauna I saw:

_____

_____

_____

_____

What I liked most about this Trip:

_____

_____

_____

_____

_____

Date of Trip:	Location of Campsite:	
	Park Name_____	
	Campground Name_____	
	Campsite Number_____	
	City/State_____	

Weather:	Mileage:	Expenses:
☀ ⛅ ☔ ❄	Today's Beginning Mileage_____ Today's Ending Mileage_____ Total Miles Driven_____	Gas $_____ Food $_____ Supplies $_____ Other $_____

Campground Details:

_____

_____

_____

_____

_____

Campsite Details:

_____

_____

_____

_____

_____

_____

_____

Activities Offered:

_____

_____

_____

_____

Things I did:

_____

_____

_____

_____

Flora and Fauna I saw:

_____

_____

_____

_____

What I liked most about this Trip:

_____

_____

_____

_____

Date of Trip:	Location of Campsite:	
	Park Name_____	
	Campground Name_____	
	Campsite Number_____	
	City/State_____	

Weather:	Mileage:	Expenses:
☀ ⛅ ☔ ❄	Today's Beginning Mileage_____ Today's Ending Mileage_____ Total Miles Driven_____	Gas $_____ Food $_____ Supplies $_____ Other $_____

Campground Details:

_____

_____

_____

_____

_____

Campsite Details:

_____

_____

_____

_____

_____

_____

_____

Activities Offered:

_____

_____

_____

_____

_____

Things I did:

_____

_____

_____

_____

Flora and Fauna I saw:

_____

_____

_____

_____

What I liked most about this Trip:

_____

_____

_____

_____

Date of Trip:	Location of Campsite:	
	Park Name_____	
	Campground Name_____	
	Campsite Number_____	
	City/State_____	

Weather:	Mileage:	Expenses:
☀ ⛅ ☁🌧 ☁❄	Today's Beginning Mileage_____ Today's Ending Mileage_____ Total Miles Driven_____	Gas $_____ Food $_____ Supplies $_____ Other $_____

Campground Details:

_____

_____

_____

_____

_____

Campsite Details:

_____

_____

_____

_____

_____

_____

_____

Activities Offered:

_____

_____

_____

_____

Things I did:

_____

_____

_____

_____

Flora and Fauna I saw:

_____

_____

_____

_____

What I liked most about this Trip:

_____

_____

_____

_____

Date of Trip:	Location of Campsite:
	Park Name_____
	Campground Name_____
	Campsite Number_____
	City/State_____

Weather:	Mileage:	Expenses:
☀ ⛅ ☔ ☂	Today's Beginning Mileage_____ Today's Ending Mileage_____ Total Miles Driven_____	Gas $_____ Food $_____ Supplies $_____ Other $_____

Campground Details:

_____

_____

_____

_____

_____

Campsite Details:

_____

_____

_____

_____

_____

_____

_____

Activities Offered:

_____

_____

_____

_____

_____

Things I did:

_____

_____

_____

_____

_____

Flora and Fauna I saw:

_____

_____

_____

_____

_____

What I liked most about this Trip:

_____

_____

_____

_____

_____

Date of Trip:	Location of Campsite:
	Park Name_____
	Campground Name_____
	Campsite Number_____
	City/State_____

Weather:	Mileage:	Expenses:
☀ ⛅ 🌧 🌨	Today's Beginning Mileage_____ Today's Ending Mileage_____ Total Miles Driven_____	Gas $_____ Food $_____ Supplies $_____ Other $_____

Campground Details:

_____

_____

_____

_____

_____

Campsite Details:

_____

_____

_____

_____

_____

_____

_____

Activities Offered:

_____

_____

_____

_____

Things I did:

_____

_____

_____

_____

Flora and Fauna I saw:

_____

_____

_____

_____

What I liked most about this Trip:

_____

_____

_____

_____

Date of Trip:	Location of Campsite: Park Name_____ Campground Name_____ Campsite Number_____ City/State_____	
Weather: ☀ ⛅ 🌧 🌨	Mileage: Today's Beginning Mileage_____ Today's Ending Mileage_____ Total Miles Driven_____	Expenses: Gas $_____ Food $_____ Supplies $_____ Other $_____

Campground Details:

_____

_____

_____

_____

_____

Campsite Details:

_____

_____

_____

_____

_____

_____

_____

Activities Offered:

_____

_____

_____

_____

Things I did:

_____

_____

_____

_____

Flora and Fauna I saw:

_____

_____

_____

_____

What I liked most about this Trip:

_____

_____

_____

_____

Date of Trip:	Location of Campsite:
	Park Name_____
	Campground Name_____
	Campsite Number_____
	City/State_____

Weather:	Mileage:	Expenses:
☀ ⛅ 🌧 🌨	Today's Beginning Mileage_____	Gas $_____
	Today's Ending Mileage_____	Food $_____
	Total Miles Driven_____	Supplies $_____
		Other $_____

Campground Details:

_____

_____

_____

_____

_____

Campsite Details:

_____

_____

_____

_____

_____

_____

_____

Activities Offered:

_____

_____

_____

_____

_____

Things I did:

_____

_____

_____

_____

_____

Flora and Fauna I saw:

_____

_____

_____

_____

_____

What I liked most about this Trip:

_____

_____

_____

_____

_____

Date of Trip:	Location of Campsite:
	Park Name_____
	Campground Name_____
	Campsite Number_____
	City/State_____

Weather:	Mileage:	Expenses:
☀ ⛅ 🌧 🌨	Today's Beginning Mileage_____ Today's Ending Mileage_____ Total Miles Driven_____	Gas $_____ Food $_____ Supplies $_____ Other $_____

Campground Details:

_____
_____
_____
_____
_____

Campsite Details:

_____
_____
_____
_____
_____
_____
_____
_____

Activities Offered:

_____

_____

_____

_____

Things I did:

_____

_____

_____

_____

Flora and Fauna I saw:

_____

_____

_____

_____

What I liked most about this Trip:

_____

_____

_____

_____

Date of Trip:	Location of Campsite:
	Park Name_____
	Campground Name_____
	Campsite Number_____
	City/State_____

Weather:	Mileage:	Expenses:
☀ ⛅ 🌧 🌨	Today's Beginning Mileage_____	Gas $_____
	Today's Ending Mileage_____	Food $_____
	Total Miles Driven_____	Supplies $_____
		Other $_____

Campground Details:

_____

_____

_____

_____

_____

Campsite Details:

_____

_____

_____

_____

_____

_____

Activities Offered:

_____

_____

_____

_____

Things I did:

_____

_____

_____

_____

Flora and Fauna I saw:

_____

_____

_____

_____

What I liked most about this Trip:

_____

_____

_____

_____

Date of Trip:	Location of Campsite:	
	Park Name_____	
	Campground Name_____	
	Campsite Number_____	
	City/State_____	

Weather:	Mileage:	Expenses:
☀ ⛅ 🌧 🌨	Today's Beginning Mileage_____ Today's Ending Mileage_____ Total Miles Driven_____	Gas $_____ Food $_____ Supplies $_____ Other $_____

Campground Details:

_____

_____

_____

_____

_____

Campsite Details:

_____

_____

_____

_____

_____

_____

_____

Activities Offered:

_____

_____

_____

_____

Things I did:

_____

_____

_____

_____

Flora and Fauna I saw:

_____

_____

_____

_____

What I liked most about this Trip:

_____

_____

_____

_____

_____

Date of Trip:	Location of Campsite:	
	Park Name_____	
	Campground Name_____	
	Campsite Number_____	
	City/State_____	

Weather:	Mileage:	Expenses:
☀ ⛅ 🌧 🌨	Today's Beginning Mileage_____ Today's Ending Mileage_____ Total Miles Driven_____	Gas $_____ Food $_____ Supplies $_____ Other $_____

Campground Details:

_____

_____

_____

_____

_____

Campsite Details:

_____

_____

_____

_____

_____

_____

_____

Activities Offered:

_____

_____

_____

_____

_____

Things I did:

_____

_____

_____

_____

Flora and Fauna I saw:

_____

_____

_____

_____

What I liked most about this Trip:

_____

_____

_____

_____

_____

Date of Trip:	Location of Campsite:
	Park Name_____
	Campground Name_____
	Campsite Number_____
	City/State_____

Weather:	Mileage:	Expenses:
☀ ⛅ ☔ ☃	Today's Beginning Mileage_____	Gas $_____
	Today's Ending Mileage_____	Food $_____
	Total Miles Driven_____	Supplies $_____
		Other $_____

Campground Details:

_____

_____

_____

_____

_____

_____

Campsite Details:

_____

_____

_____

_____

_____

_____

_____

Activities Offered:

_____

_____

_____

_____

Things I did:

_____

_____

_____

_____

Flora and Fauna I saw:

_____

_____

_____

_____

What I liked most about this Trip:

_____

_____

_____

_____

_____

Date of Trip:	Location of Campsite:
	Park Name_____
	Campground Name_____
	Campsite Number_____
	City/State_____

Weather:	Mileage:	Expenses:
☀ ⛅ 🌧 🌨	Today's Beginning Mileage_____ Today's Ending Mileage_____ Total Miles Driven_____	Gas $_____ Food $_____ Supplies $_____ Other $_____

Campground Details:

_____

_____

_____

_____

_____

Campsite Details:

_____

_____

_____

_____

_____

_____

_____

Activities Offered:

_____

_____

_____

_____

Things I did:

_____

_____

_____

_____

Flora and Fauna I saw:

_____

_____

_____

_____

What I liked most about this Trip:

_____

_____

_____

_____

_____

Date of Trip:	Location of Campsite:
	Park Name_____
	Campground Name_____
	Campsite Number_____
	City/State_____

Weather:	Mileage:	Expenses:
☀ ⛅ ☁🌧 🌨	Today's Beginning Mileage_____ Today's Ending Mileage_____ Total Miles Driven_____	Gas $_____ Food $_____ Supplies $_____ Other $_____

Campground Details:

_____
_____
_____
_____
_____

Campsite Details:

_____
_____
_____
_____
_____
_____
_____

Activities Offered:

_____

_____

_____

_____

Things I did:

_____

_____

_____

_____

Flora and Fauna I saw:

_____

_____

_____

_____

What I liked most about this Trip:

_____

_____

_____

_____

_____

Date of Trip:	Location of Campsite:	
	Park Name_____	
	Campground Name_____	
	Campsite Number_____	
	City/State_____	

Weather:	Mileage:	Expenses:
☀ ⛅ 🌧 🌨	Today's Beginning Mileage_____ Today's Ending Mileage_____ Total Miles Driven_____	Gas $_____ Food $_____ Supplies $_____ Other $_____

Campground Details:

_____

_____

_____

_____

_____

Campsite Details:

_____

_____

_____

_____

_____

_____

_____

Activities Offered:

_____

_____

_____

_____

_____

Things I did:

_____

_____

_____

_____

_____

Flora and Fauna I saw:

_____

_____

_____

_____

_____

What I liked most about this Trip:

_____

_____

_____

_____

_____

_____

Date of Trip:	Location of Campsite:
	Park Name_____
	Campground Name_____
	Campsite Number_____
	City/State_____

Weather:	Mileage:	Expenses:
☀ ⛅	Today's Beginning Mileage_____	Gas $_____
🌧 🌨	Today's Ending Mileage_____	Food $_____
	Total Miles Driven_____	Supplies $_____
		Other $_____

Campground Details:

_____

_____

_____

_____

_____

_____

Campsite Details:

_____

_____

_____

_____

_____

_____

_____

Activities Offered:

_____

_____

_____

_____

Things I did:

_____

_____

_____

_____

Flora and Fauna I saw:

_____

_____

_____

_____

What I liked most about this Trip:

_____

_____

_____

_____

_____

Date of Trip:	Location of Campsite:
	Park Name_____
	Campground Name_____
	Campsite Number_____
	City/State_____

Weather:	Mileage:	Expenses:
☀ ⛅ ☁ ☔	Today's Beginning Mileage_____ Today's Ending Mileage_____ Total Miles Driven_____	Gas $_____ Food $_____ Supplies $_____ Other $_____

Campground Details:

_____

_____

_____

_____

_____

Campsite Details:

_____

_____

_____

_____

_____

_____

_____

Activities Offered:

_____

_____

_____

_____

_____

Things I did:

_____

_____

_____

_____

_____

Flora and Fauna I saw:

_____

_____

_____

_____

_____

What I liked most about this Trip:

_____

_____

_____

_____

_____

Date of Trip:	Location of Campsite:
	Park Name_____
	Campground Name_____
	Campsite Number_____
	City/State_____

Weather:	Mileage:	Expenses:
☀ ⛅ 🌧 🌨	Today's Beginning Mileage_____	Gas $_____
	Today's Ending Mileage_____	Food $_____
	Total Miles Driven_____	Supplies $_____
		Other $_____

Campground Details:

_____

_____

_____

_____

_____

Campsite Details:

_____

_____

_____

_____

_____

_____

Activities Offered:

_____

_____

_____

_____

Things I did:

_____

_____

_____

_____

Flora and Fauna I saw:

_____

_____

_____

_____

What I liked most about this Trip:

_____

_____

_____

_____

_____

Date of Trip:	Location of Campsite:
	Park Name_____
	Campground Name_____
	Campsite Number_____
	City/State_____

Weather:	Mileage:	Expenses:
☀ ⛅ ☔ ❄	Today's Beginning Mileage_____ Today's Ending Mileage_____ Total Miles Driven_____	Gas $_____ Food $_____ Supplies $_____ Other $_____

Campground Details:

_____

_____

_____

_____

_____

Campsite Details:

_____

_____

_____

_____

_____

_____

Activities Offered:

_____

_____

_____

_____

Things I did:

_____

_____

_____

_____

Flora and Fauna I saw:

_____

_____

_____

_____

What I liked most about this Trip:

_____

_____

_____

_____

If you enjoyed this journal, we have many more styles and types to choose from. Visit our website for a complete list of journals.

www.wanderingwalksofwonder.com

National Parks Exploration Journal

My Bucket List Journal

Road Trip Journal

50 State Travel Journal

62815608R00057

Made in the USA
Lexington, KY
18 April 2017